50 STATES FACTS & FUN

VIKI WOODWORTH

DOVER PUBLICATIONS, INC.
MINEOLA, NEW YORK

Bibliographical Note

The 50 States: Facts & Fun is a new work, first published by Dover Publications, Inc., in 2010.

International Standard Book Number
ISBN-13: 978-0-486-47524-0
ISBN-10: 0-486-47524-7

Manufactured in the United States by Courier Corporation
47524701
www.doverpublications.com

Note

It's impossible to find all of the fantastic facts about the United States in one place—but this fun-filled book has dozens of them! You'll learn something about each state as you enjoy using codes, doing word searches and crosswords, solving mazes, and even drawing your own pictures. From north to south and from east to west, every state is included. (Many of the state names are mentioned in the captions, but some are found only in the solutions.) Are you ready for some facts and fun? Let's get started!

the color of 🍌 **+** 🔨

The **Alabama** state bird is a type of woodpecker. Its name is made up of two words put together as one. To figure out this name, use the picture clues and fill in the blanks.

5

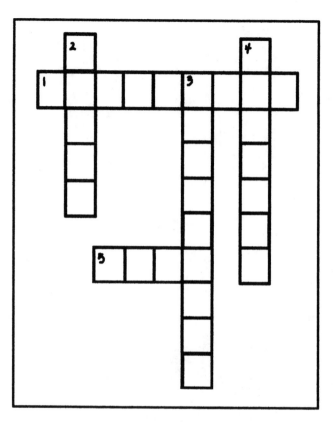

Alaska is known as the "Last Frontier." Use the picture clues on the opposite page to fill in the crossword blanks.

The number next to each picture about **Alaska** tells you where the word belongs in the puzzle.

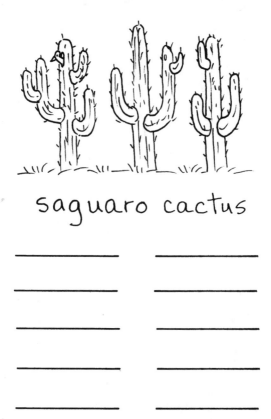

saguaro cactus

——————— ———————

——————— ———————

——————— ———————

——————— ———————

——————— ———————

The Saguaro cactus grows in the deserts of **Arizona.**
Fill in the blanks with as many words as you can,
using the letters in the words SAGUARO CACTUS. You
can use a separate paper to write more words.

Many chickens and eggs come from **Arkansas.** Each of the chickens above lays a different type of egg. Count each chicken's eggs, and write the number on the line. Put an X next to the chicken with the most eggs.

9

Colorado has many enormous mountains. To find out the name of the mountain range above, write the word that goes with each picture in the blanks. The letters in the circles spell out the name.

10

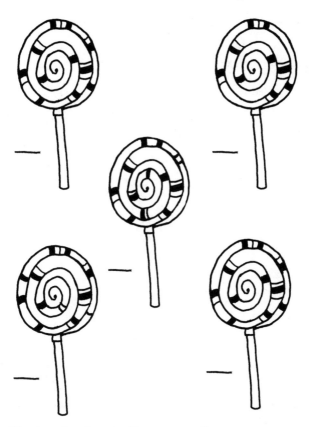

Here's a fun fact: Lollipops were first created in the state of **Connecticut.** Put an X next to the two lollipops that are exactly the same.

The state bird of **Delaware** is the Blue Hen Chicken. Connect the dots to see its picture.

12

States such as **Iowa, Illinois, Indiana, Nebraska,** and **Kansas** have many farms. Circle the seven things in this picture that you would *not* see on a farm.

Florida is the home of the Kennedy Space Center. One spacecraft is ready to take off. It has three stripes and one dot. Find and circle this spacecraft.

14

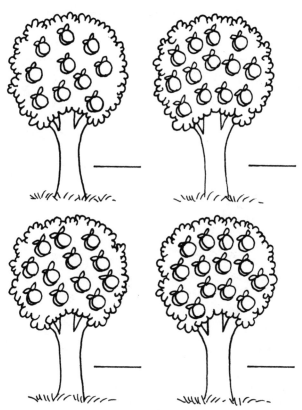

There are many peach trees in **Georgia.** Count the peaches on each tree and write the number in the blank next to it. Then circle the tree with the most peaches. Put an X on the tree that has the fewest.

15

Pineapples, sugar cane, and macadamia nuts grow in **Hawaii.** David has one pineapple, three pieces of sugar cane, and four macadamia nuts. Put an X on David's square.

16

Idaho is famous for its potatoes. Jake, Maria, Jen, and Matt have a favorite type of potato. Write the number of each potato favorite on the correct dinner plate.

2 stripes
3 dots
3 squares

1 stripe
3 dots
2 squares

4 stripes
3 dots
2 squares

3 stripes
2 dots
2 squares

Several popcorn festivals are held in **Indiana.** Each of these children has a special bowl of popcorn. Draw a line from each child to the bowl that matches the description.

The "World's Largest Ball of Twine" can be found in Cawker City, **Kansas.** One of these children is holding on to the end of the twine. Find and circle that child.

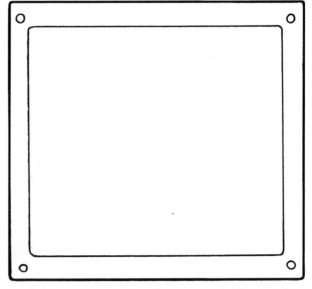

Each of the fifty states has its own special license plate design. Have fun designing your own license plate in the space above. Don't forget to include the name of your state.

The Brown Pelican is the state bird of **Louisiana.** Help this pelican find its way to the end of the lagoon. In the blank, write how many fish it catches along the way.

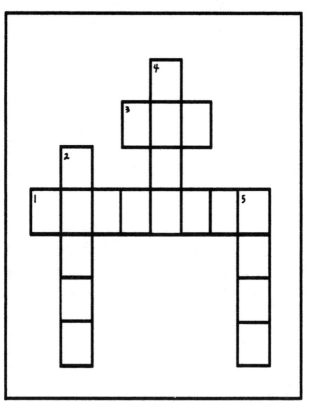

The names of several things that the state of **Maine** is known for are the answers to this crossword puzzle. Use the picture clues on the opposite page to fill in the blanks.

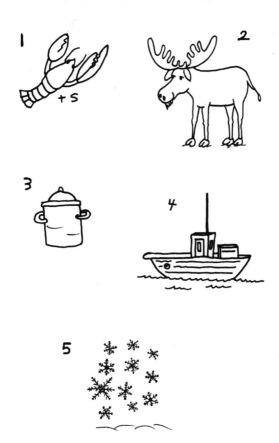

The number next to each picture about **Maine** tells you where the word belongs in the puzzle. Clues 1 and 3 together tell about one thing.

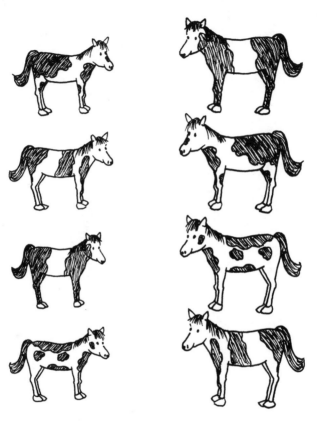

Maryland is the home of Assateague Island, where wild ponies live. Each mother pony has a matching baby pony. Draw a line from each baby to its mother.

Lake _____

Lake Chargoggagoggmanchauggagoggchaubunag-
ungamaugg is in **Massachusetts.** If you could name a
lake, what would you call it? Write it in the blank, and
draw some plants and animals in your picture, too.

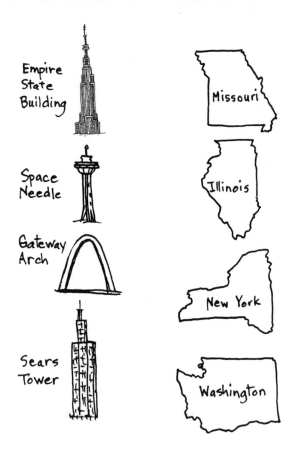

Empire State Building

Space Needle

Gateway Arch

Sears Tower

Missouri

Illinois

New York

Washington

Draw a line matching each famous landmark on the left to the state where it can be found on the right.

P	S	O	X	C	Q	R	W	T	U	A	D
M	C	A	L	I	F	O	R	N	I	A	U
Z	N	R	Q	J	T	S	W	E	B	Y	Z
S	B	I	K	C	L	Z	E	W	I	O	F
G	W	Z	V	N	F	X	D	M	D	H	M
X	Y	O	P	M	R	P	G	E	U	C	I
Q	A	N	U	O	A	T	E	X	A	S	C
B	D	A	T	Q	Z	I	Y	I	Q	F	B
N	E	I	B	J	S	V	N	C	E	K	R
O	H	P	L	X	A	W	H	O	R	G	V
F	C	D	H	C	V	G	E	A	I	P	S

TEXAS   NEW MEXICO
CALIFORNIA   ARIZONA

The names of the four states that border Mexico are hidden in this puzzle. Find and circle the four state names.

CODE

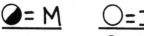

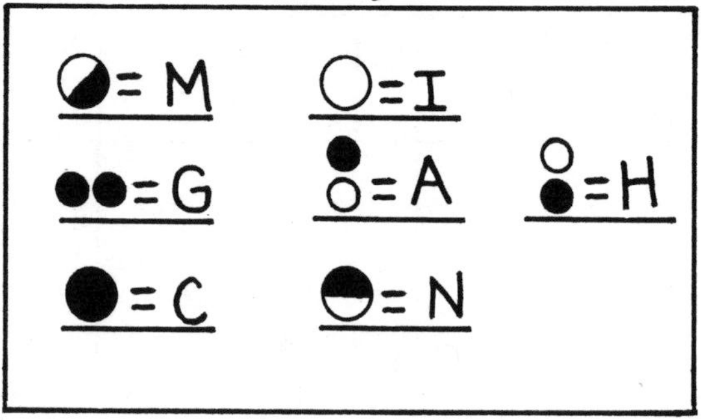

◐ = M	◯ = I	
●● = G	� = A	🌑 = H
● = C	◓ = N	

— — — — — — — —

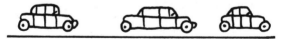

Which state is famous for making cars? Use the shape code to spell out the name of this state. Write the letters where they belong in the blanks.

The state bird of **Minnesota** is the Common Loon. Show the mother loon the path she needs to take to reach her baby at the end.

steamboat

_____   _____

_____   _____

_____   _____

_____   _____

_____   _____

Steamboats can pass through these ten states as they travel on the Mississippi River: **Minnesota, Wisconsin, Iowa, Illinois, Missouri, Kentucky, Tennessee, Arkansas, Mississippi,** and **Louisiana.** How many words can you make from STEAMBOAT? Write them on the lines. You can use a separate paper to write more words.

Grizzly bears live in **Montana** and in other western states. Connect the dots above to see a picture of a grizzly.

31

Many states hold a state fair every year. The **Nevada** State Fair features a Wiener Dog Race. Can you spot six differences between this page and the one opposite?

Find and put an X on the six differences.

Figure the Code

🐕 = ☐   🐙 = ☐

🍎 = ☐   🌳 = ☐

🪁 = ☐   🥕 = ☐

▥ = ☐   🦁 = ☐

🐢 = ☐   🪹 = ☐

Did you know that two state names begin with "North" and two begin with "South"? To figure out the code, write the first letter of each item above in the box.

34

North and South

___ ___ ___ ___ ___ ___ ___ ___

___ ___ ___ ___ ___ ___ ___

North and South

___ ___ ___ ___ ___ ___

Now use the code to write the names of the "North" and "South" state names.

Salt-water taffy was first made in **New Jersey.** Sarah has the spotted pieces, and Sam has the striped ones. Count how many pieces each child has and write the number on the line. Who has more? Circle the number.

36

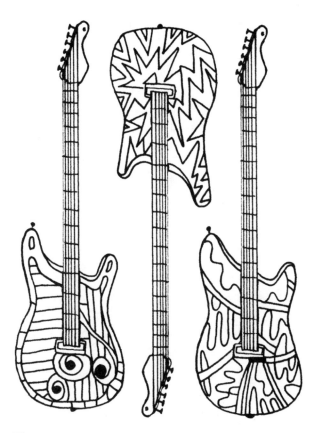

The Rock and Roll Hall of Fame is located in Cleveland, **Ohio.** You can see decorated electric guitars belonging to famous rock musicians there.

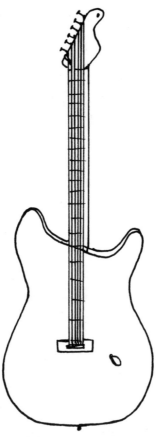

Here's your chance to decorate your own electric guitar!

38

Pioneers traveled west on the Oregon Trail. The trail started in Independence, **Missouri,** and ended in **Oregon.** Help this pioneer wagon make its way to the end of the trail.

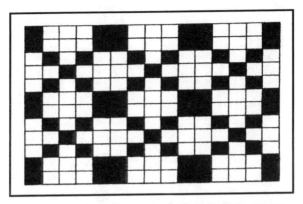

Some states, such as **Pennsylvania, Virginia,** and **West Virginia,** are known for their beautifully designed quilts. Quilts usually are made using many fabric squares of different colors and patterns.

40

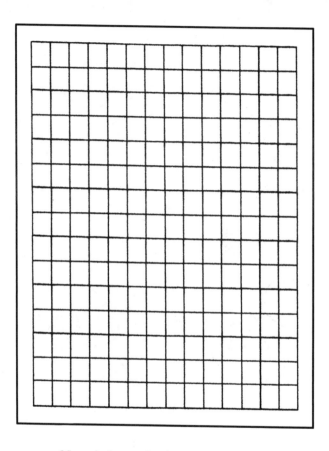

Now design and color your own quilt!

The first official celebration of Groundhog Day, February 2, took place in Punxsutawney, **Pennsylvania.** Which tunnel will lead this groundhog home? Follow the path and circle the number of the correct tunnel.

Johnny cakes, also known as jonnycakes, are a type of cornmeal pancake from **Rhode Island.** Look carefully at the stacks of Johnny cakes. Then circle the two stacks that are exactly the same.

S I T T W

___ ___ ___ ___ ___

The singer Chubby Checker, born in **South Carolina,** invented a famous dance in the 1960s. Unscramble the letters to find the name of this dance. Write the answer in the blanks.

S	X	P	O	C	Q	W	T	R	A	U	D
N	J	E	F	F	E	R	S	O	N	G	Z
G	K	R	T	H	N	G	W	O	V	Y	U
S	O	F	U	L	T	Z	T	U	G	N	I
Z	E	V	G	R	D	G	H	N	P	H	C
M	B	E	L	I	N	C	O	L	N	O	M
Q	Z	O	U	I	J	S	P	Q	D	F	B
X	D	B	H	R	X	Y	H	B	K	K	S
N	E	S	P	K	B	Q	S	I	R	A	V
O	A	R	O	O	S	E	V	E	L	T	R
W	C	H	V	G	A	I	P	S	H	D	F

THEODORE ROOSEVELT   ABRAHAM LINCOLN
GEORGE WASHINGTON   THOMAS JEFFERSON

The faces of four presidents are carved into Mount Rushmore, **South Dakota.** Find and circle the last names of the four presidents in the puzzle.

45

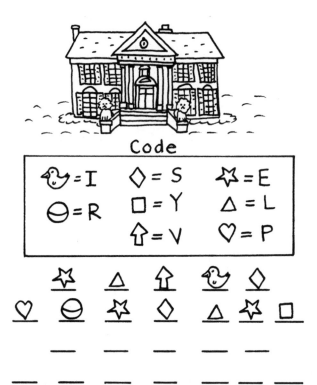

Code

🐦 = I   ◇ = S   ☆ = E

⊖ = R   □ = Y   △ = L

⇧ = V   ♡ = P

☆ △ ⇧ 🐦 ◇

_ _ _ _ _

♡ ⊖ ☆ ◇ △ ☆ □

_ _ _ _ _ _ _

Graceland, in Memphis, **Tennessee,** was the home of a famous singer. Use the code to figure out his name. Then write it in the blanks.

46

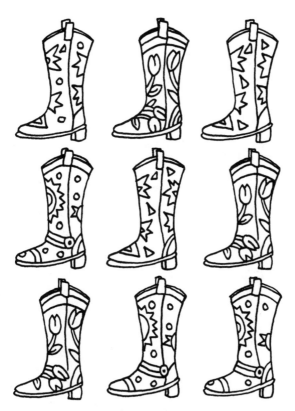

Many people in **Texas** and **Oklahoma** and other western states wear cowboy boots. Look carefully at the boots above and circle the two that are exactly the same.

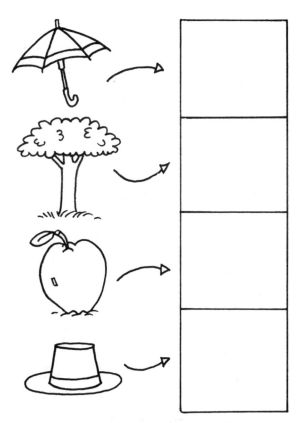

Which state is the home of the Great Salt Lake, which is so salty that you can float in it? Write the first letter of each picture in the boxes to spell the state's name.

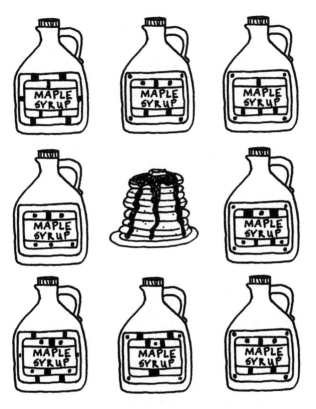

The states of **Vermont** and **New Hampshire** are known for producing maple syrup. Take a good look at the jugs of maple syrup and circle the two that are exactly the same.

49

A famous story about a "Jackalope" comes from the
state of **Wyoming.** The Jackalope is a made-up creature
that is part jackrabbit and part antelope.

50

Now invent a creature of your own. Think of two animals you can combine, and then draw a picture. For example, it could be a pig and a dog—a "pog." Have fun!

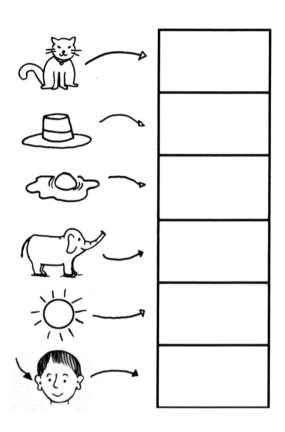

Wisconsin is famous for making this popular food item. Write the first letter of each picture in the boxes to spell the item's name.

SOLUTIONS

page 5

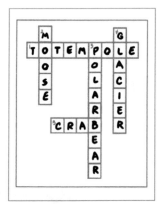

page 6

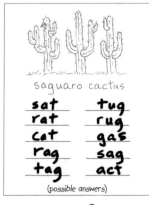

page 8

page 9

54

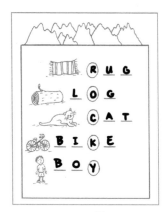

page 10

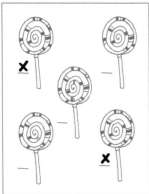

page 11

page 12

page 13

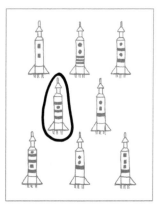

page 14

page 15

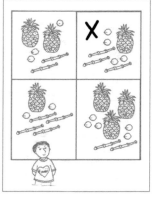

page 16

page 17

page 18

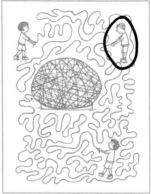

page 19

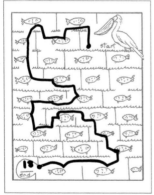

page 21

page 22

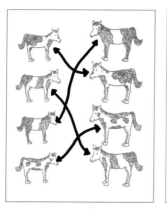

page 24

page 26

TEXAS   NEW MEXICO
CALIFORNIA   ARIZONA

page 27

CODE

◑ = M   ○ = I   ◓ = A   ◒ = H
●● = G   ● = C   ◐ = N

M I C H I G A N

page 28

58

page 29

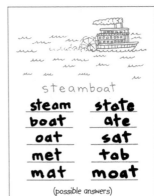

page 30

page 31

page 33

Figure the Code

🐕 = **D**			🐙 = **O**
🍎 = **A**			🌳 = **T**
🪁 = **K**			🥕 = **C**
🎀 = **R**			🦁 = **L**
🐢 = **I**			🪺 = **N**

page 34

North and South

C A R O L I N A

North and South

D A K O T A

page 35

page 36

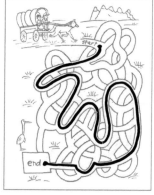

page 39

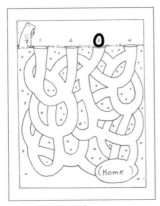

page 42

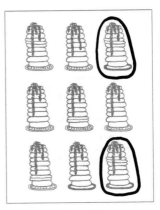

page 43

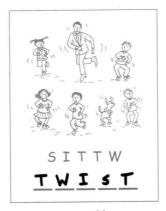

page 44

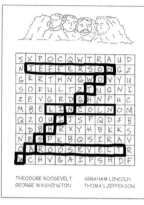

page 45

THEODORE ROOSEVELT   ABRAHAM LINCOLN
GEORGE WASHINGTON   THOMAS JEFFERSON

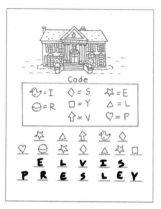

page 46

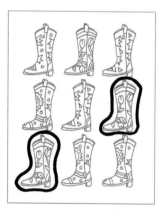

page 47

page 48

page 49

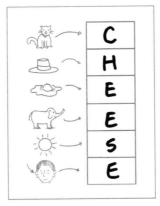

page 52